SECOND INNINGS

THE TURNING POINT

SECOND INNINGS
THE TURNING POINT

AUTHORED BY

CHITRA SEN

Penman Books

Office No. 303, Kumar House Building,
D Block, Central Market, Opp PVR Cinema,
Prashant Vihar, Delhi 110085, India
Website: www.penmanbooks.com
Email: publish@penmanbooks.com

First Published by Penman Books 2020
Copyright © Chitra Sen 2020
All Rights Reserved.

Title: Second Innings
Price: ₹ 499 | $ 9
ISBN: 978-93-89024-74-6

ACKNOWLEDGEMENTS

This book is dedicated to my family - my husband Deepak Kumar Sen who always inspired me to march forward in life; my daughters Shahana and Chandana, my son-in-laws Shivashish and Vipin, my grand children Siddhant, Arnab, Mira and Karan who were the foundations of my launchpad; and a special thanks to my daughter-in-law Anita who made me realize my dream.

A million thanks to you too, Arfeen Khan, my mentor and guide, for your inspiration, drive and guidance all the way.

My fellow Toastmasters, friends, the book club members, coaches at mastermind - all those have contributed to my thoughts in their own ways - a big Thank You.

I must also thank all those who made a difference in my life and made this dream come true through their individual contributions which helped me in my journey towards writing this book.

In the end, I must thank my publishers Kailash Pinjani and Dr. Deepak Vilas Parbat of Penman Books for their invaluable assistance and advice in the structuring of this book.

FOREWORD

Our earliest memories of her, our Aunt (fondly called 'Kakima') are those of a vivacious, happy-go-lucky person, eager to savour life to its fullest! She has never been one to shy away from new adventures, novel experiences or unexpected challenges - she has reinvented herself many a time over.

This book is a fun memoir typical of the author, a delightful slice of a life lived to the full, narrated with a keen eye to the future, ready for new journeys.

Her boundless enthusiasm and unfettered joie-de-vivre infect everyone who associates with her, and the same energy is evident in good measure in this book. So enjoy it, dear readers, and light up your spark of self-discovery.

Drs Arun & Aneeta Sen
Newcastle - upon - Tyne (UK)
27 Jan 2020

PREFACE

In my life I have sometimes come across people who have many regrets due to their way of thinking, as a result of which they had to encounter insurmountable obstacles and heartbreaks. Now that I look back, I too have faced many such ups and downs. The way you deal with the existing situation and the perception change required at that time - how you think and ultimately tackle the problem - is a lesson to learn. I therefore thought of penning down some of my thinking and problem solving processes so that others may benefit from that knowledge and avoid the disappointments and sense of insecurity that I sometimes had to experience and overcome. Now that I have become a Transformational Coach after having gone through the break-through process myself, I want to touch many other lives with the intention of empowering them also to lead a meaningful existence and achieve success. My own experience as an ordinary individual, which I have penned down in the book, may help to make the difference in their lives.

CONTENTS

CHAPTER ONE

ME AND MY STORY

The proverb 'rolling stones gather no moss' may have many connotations, but to me, it meant a life full of new experiences, newer visions, and to truly capture the essence of life.

God created little Chitra on a roller coaster, born to a family of working parents with my father away from home most of the time. As far as I can recall, my mother often moved houses and places at short intervals every time as the lease of the house would get over due to rent disagreement or trying to find homes near her workplace. Though I was born on a Laxmi Puja day, the goddess has played many pranks with me since then where wealth is concerned, and yet it is a blessing that she has always kept my neck above water. Being the only child I was predictably pampered, and since my mother was working, my creche was always full of relatives and extended members of the family. My growing up days as far as I can recall followed a rhythmic pattern. The turning point in my life was when my father, who was a foreign correspondence of a leading newspaper in Kolkata took us to England. The influx of Indians had just started during the 1960s. My stay in England was flavoured with new experiences and new learning, making new friends and bonding with children of different nationalities. Eventually, I went to study in a hill station tucked away in the Himalayas. The only stability I had was during mid-school and college, where I was secured within the walls of a convent with girls from all over the world. Along with discipline, I experienced the joy of growing up with girls of my age from different backgrounds and homes. The upbringing we got in our alma mater is relatively redundant now. Girls were taught to be polite, sit cross-legged to be demure and were taught to be articulate, played games, learned fine arts all in a measured way.

Even though discipline ruled our lives, this part of growing up was fun-filled, playing pranks with classmates and teachers, having midnight parties in the dormitories, taking part in debates, annual days and, of course, planning eagerly for the annual prom dance under the vigilant eyes of the black-veiled nuns. Those were the best years of my life when I made life-long friends. Even now, whenever we meet at school reunions, we regale the past with gusto, tinted with nostalgia. When each academic year came to an end with its tiresome routine of studies and exams, it would be time for the holidays and to go home. Little did I know that packing the black trunks at that time would play a great role later in my life.

My college life was also walled; the College had its own set of rules. That notwithstanding, as a young girl I did have my share of fun too - bunking classes, going to the coffee house, mixing with university seniors, dabbling in politics secretly (since it was a turbulent period in Bengal politics).

Most of the girls in my college were cookie-cutters; some went on for further studies while the rest walked the well-trodden path to become teachers, lawyers or joined the banks. I too, was contemplating what I should do after college. Our exams got postponed indefinitely due to the growing Naxalite agitation, and the vacuum was filled by getting hit by Cupid's arrows. I was smitten by the man in uniform.

As the set routine of school and college ended, I embarked on the second phase of my life at an early age, with tinted celluloid dreams of seeing Rajesh Khanna as an Air Force officer yodelling in an open jeep. I soon joined the officers' club in the role of a defence officer's wife.

A whirlwind swept me across India from Kashmir to Kanyakumari, crisscrossing the length and breadth of India - from the cold mountains to the inky blue seas and arid deserts - a panorama covered which would make even travel giant Thomas Cook seem inadequate! Yet once again, my life was enclosed within the boundaries of the defence campus. While my husband managed and protected the geographical frontiers of India, we, ladies of the Defense Forces and the unsung heroes, managed the home fronts so that the guardians of the nation did not have to wear a wrinkle on their brows.

My life was enriched, interacting with the rank and file of people from different states and cultures. Being a single child, I was embraced into a large cosmopolitan family. There was never a dull moment from learning to flavour different cuisine or celebrating a variety of religious, cultural festivities with equal gusto. The calendar was always dotted with red ink. Casseroles were exchanged with Mrs. Iyer's sambar to Mrs Ahmed's biryani which would often adorn the dinner table. Learning, discovering, having new experiences, was a never-ending process.

My daughters and I would eagerly await every block year for the announcement of posting orders, and with unfailing regularity, my husband would announce in his baritone, 'It's time to pack up'. Out came the small, big trunks and wooden boxes; the whole family with experienced deft fingers would start labelling all the drawing-room, kitchen and other articles in boxes of various sizes. With each posting, we became smarter and wiser. Same sized boxes would become our beds, tea roots from the tea estates would be transformed into tables. A piece of driftwood from the river Torsa would adorn the drawing-room.

The years that we were lucky to have postings at various Command Headquarters, I would seize the opportunity to add on to degrees, certificates and diplomas to satisfy my intellectual quest. Being married early, there were times when my daughters Shona, Rupa and I grew up together, studied, discovered new things and kinship grew where we learned to share a wonderful camaraderie that has remained in our life so far. We would prepare for competitive exams at the same time, while my husband made umpteen cups of coffee to keep us awake. My father in law would always listen patiently to our monotonous revisions with discerning eyes and the ever-present knowing smile, clarifying any doubts that we had during our preparation.

Whenever opportunity knocked my way, I seized it to enable myself to keep abreast with the fast-moving world. During this period, Goddess Saraswati often conspired against me by taking long and unexpected sabbaticals. When man and God conspire against you, it is better to go with the flow. Though my career graph shows short, interrupted stints, I can boast of referrals from all over the country.

As life whizzed past me in a jiffy, constantly traversing the length and breadth of the globe, packing, unpacking and living under different roofs from thatched roof 'Bashas' in Assam, where we would have to clutch the rooftop on a stormy night to prevent it from flying, moving in barracks, transit camps, temporary quarters, to sprawling bungalows with manicured lawns in Akbar Road - I could, in fact, write a ready reckoner on housing for any well-known builder!

One fine day as I started to sum up my life of adventure, meeting people, making friends, some parts of it faded in the depths of memory - so many trivialities of life, unfulfilled aspirations, kept and un-kept promises fluttered through my mind. But then, life for me never stood still.

At last, as per the dictates of time, the stage was set for the last bugle call, but my husband was not ready to hang up his boots yet. The familiar tone said 'march on', and out came the boxes, but this time with a difference. The rattling olive green one tonner was replaced by the brightly coloured Agarwal Packers load carrier and instead of black trunks and irregular boxes, there were neat piles of brown cartons containing souvenirs, medals, trophies, memorabilia, remnants of our rich and varied life, all transported lock, stock and barrel to this part of India which was to be our next home. It is often said that life is a full circle. My dears, it all started here in this beautiful city of Bangalore, where I presently reside. I met my husband - at that time a cadet under training with crew hair cut and curled moustaches - at the Jalahalli AFTC Officers' Mess in Bangalore - and I was the wide-eyed tourist on a trip, discovering South India and life and living!

Well, that is life, so akin to Nature, ever-changing, beautiful, captivating, mysterious and at the same time somewhat frightening because of the unknown. It is perhaps because of this nature of life that it is such a precious experience. And so it is said -

> *Life is not a barrel of laughs;*
> *It is one laugh at a time—*
> *You must assemble your own barrel*
> *And put the laughs in as you progress.*

So here I am, raising a toast to myself saying 'Cheers' to the Second Innings!

My life, which has been like a roller coaster ride for the most part, is living testimony to the need for a perception change and adaptability. It has helped me to mould and adapt myself to changing situations and environments, survive and live life happily and successfully through all the changing panorama of my existence. Indeed, if I had not done so, I may have degenerated into a depressed and discontented recluse, totally unacceptable to society.

Throughout my life, I have faced a lot of insecurity - since from my childhood, I have been shifting homes frequently. Often I felt lonely, incapable and depressed. It was then that I realized that I needed a change in my perceptions and that the change was not only necessary but also inevitable.

I then asked myself these questions along the way :

(a) Can I change myself at any age and stage in my life?

(b) Do I need to be rigid in my actions and thoughts?

(c) If a situation cannot change, can I change my perception of the situation?

(d) Shouldn't we view the world as a kaleidoscope and design our lives in a new panorama, where bits and pieces join to make a beautiful design?

(e) Did I perceive the world without awareness?

(f) Was I giving too much attention to public opinion?

(g) Am I scared of confrontation that I would have to face due to change?

(i) Can I go against my belief system?

(j) Would I behave differently?

(k) Would the new me mirror me with conviction?

CHAPTER TWO
CHANGES IN PERCEPTION

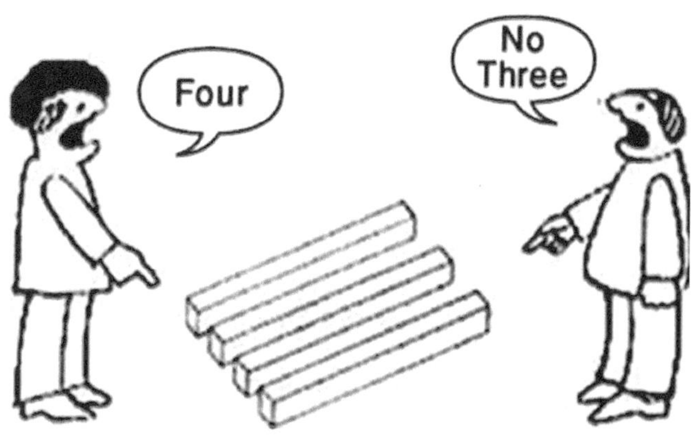

"Change will not
Come if we wait for some other time.
We are the ones we've been waiting for.
We are the change that we seek."

—**Barack Obama**

Tradition and Progression

We generally sit on things done in the past and call it 'tradition'. A tradition is generally a change brought about by usage, custom or norm as part of social interaction and acceptance over a period of time. The usage, custom or norm may take the likening of social groups or society and grow into traditional events. New thought processes can also be incorporated to create a pattern for a particular habitual, convenient and, over a period of time in a group or general interest, develop into a tradition. This process is a transitional process towards a permanent action pattern. If you go to a new place, you can form a little action pattern as required. The need to create something new also keeps flowing to new ideas and ways that we hand down from old to young and from one person to another. That is how traditions change.

Do you remember the 60s and 70s when sharing was caring, when we shared secrets with our friends in college canteens, exchanged our clothes with our siblings and friends? Discussions from politics to family gossips were held at dining tables and time was spent being at home together and sharing the day's as well as other experiences. Traditions within the family were strong and also gave strength to the enjoyment of traditional festivals like Dussehra, Holi or Diwali. Families intermingled and shared each others' experiences. The strong social institutions were undivided and singular in nature. Sharing then was traditional, based on family ties and relationships. Suddenly the world opened up, taken over by technology, glitter and devices big and small, which fascinated and tempted us to accept and explore the new world.

Today, double-income families have sprung up since the world has shrunk, and travel has become so easy. Many old traditions which were strong in the past have become obsolete. The new insurgence of Pub, Club and Mall culture, corporate work culture and associated travel have given a new dimension to social structure. The intermingling of cultures at the workplace and resulting intermarriages have given a different perspective to the status of tradition. Will this lead to the end of tradition or a change in its value system, or is this a transition of social norms and values? Is it an evolution of a new social structure or progress of the old order with material development and its usage, or is society undergoing transition all the time in sync with social behaviour influenced with the impact of technological development?

Few people write letters or send greetings any more – SMS, email, Facebook, What's App, Video Calls and a host of other applications and facilities have shrunk the world, digitized our existence and made mankind more technologically inclined than human. Everything is at the press of a button or a mouse click! Gone is the fun, pleasure and cherishing of relationships with the direct or physical process. Everyone is rushing to get more things done, with generosity, patience and understanding taking a back seat. All sharing is mostly for common interests or requirement rather than feeling. Generosity now feels so taxing. Nobody calls friends any more – instead, everybody is on the 'same page' together on on-line shopping. FaceBook activity has definitely shifted more towards materialistic pursuits rather than emotions of the heart and bonding of relationships. The concrete walls of the city have also undergone a transformation from political slogans to colourful graffiti, with necessary paints supplied by various NGOs & artists. Each era creates an identity with a tradition of its own to blossom into millions of flowers.

What is good, and what is bad? It is often only a matter of perception. If transition is a must as it appears to be in tune with everything in the universe, then traditions and hence social behaviour cannot remain constant. Perhaps it is this transition that re-kindles interest in the past, thus generating an interminable cycle of human behaviour. It appears, therefore, that what is history today will surely become a reality again, sometime in the tomorrow of our existence.

Changes in life and situations, therefore, must not be judged, but rather understood, accepted, adapted to and used for the benefit of all in life and living. Understanding, adapting to and correcting one's perceptions of life situations, therefore, play an extremely important role in the success of one's future.

To begin with, what is the definition of Perception?

Cambridge Dictionary: *a belief or opinion, often held by many people and based on how things seem*

Oxford Dictionary: *the way you notice things, especially with the senses*

Collins dictionary: *the recognition of things using your senses, especially the sense of sight*

Simply and practically stated, Perception is the process of assessing information in our environment to draw conclusions for further decision-making which directly influences our social, corporate, public or personal behaviour.

Such assessments are quite different for different individuals, depending on their individual personalities, experience and outlook. Therefore perceptions are different for different people and may also be substantially different from objective reality.

That being so, we must necessarily introspect and ensure that what we perceive is the actual reality and make corrections if necessary, so that our response in various aspects would be accurate and result in efficient, adaptable and harmonious interactions for a progressive, happy and satisfying existence.

All those who want to better their life experience must therefore look for possible changes in factors that influence perception, like our own attributes, attitudes, motives, interests, experience and expectations; prevailing situations involving time, work or social factors and the desired target in terms of novelty, background or similarity of the environment with respect to our lives. So you must go ahead and engage in a happy, adaptive perception for better living!

That is how to take life in your stride.

My life is an example of many changes in perception along the way - from an eventful childhood to the strict codes of school and college, then the quantum jump to a military society and back to civil environment where I have progressed in various professions. This journey could not have been successful without necessary and adaptive perception changes all along.

That makes me ask all of you - where do you stand? Introspect, and when you are done, ask yourself some honest questions and seek honest answers from within yourself - it will help in the perception change, which may be required for success in your future life. A change in perception may sometimes be required, because your perception of a situation is based on what you see and comprehend, and the messages that come to you from what you see and comprehend may not always be the reality.

Try to answer the questions listed below, for you to think over :

1. What are the advantages and disadvantages of transition?

2. How does Transition impact progress?

3. What do I need to leave behind?

4. Where do I want to be?

5. How do you evaluate that humans learn through evidence-based practice?

6. Why do we like to cling on to tradition?

7. Does tradition give you an identity?

8. What does perception depend on?

9. Why is it sometimes necessary to change your perception?

10. Can you think of examples where what you perceive may not be the reality?

11. Have you come across any situation in your life which has made you feel the need for a change of perception?

CHAPTER THREE
PERSISTENCE

"There's a kinship among men who have sat by a dying fire and measured the worth of their life by it."

—Sir William Golding

In life we often face victories and disastrous defeats - sometimes perhaps due to our miscalculations, inability to predict the outcome in a game of chance, where God and men have conspired against you, and the inevitable happens. What would you do then? Fall flat and remain defeated, or rave and rant and blame the whole world and for how long?

It is said that what is natural is good and therefore, go rave and rant and let off your steam, cry, lighten yourself and be empty to start afresh. Throw all the positive thinkers and advisors out of the window for the time being, because when we are feeling down and low, it is necessary to first attend to our negative feelings, for they affect our emotions too. We need not suppress them and let them erode our inner peace and judgment. One has first to let go of all that has piled up inside us.

Failure breaks a person - it is better to admit it than to falsely put up a front. We are not scared to fail but are more worried about what others would think of us if we do. Once negative feelings and old conditioning have been released, our intuitive and creative abilities are progressively given strength to grow through easy and enjoyable self-development. We begin to feel and realize who we are and understand what our deeper self really wants. We are freed from feeling trapped. Our thinking mind begins to access our higher knowing mind in achieving success.

Anything in life needs constant perseverance. Have you seen a potter at work - his constant effort of shaping and reshaping the clay and then ultimately baking it in the sun to harden the product to make it perfect?

Often we give up on the repeated efforts because it is tiresome to do the same thing again and again. Recently I had undergone a surgery where I had to learn to walk again doing all the things that I had done earlier like a baby who has to learn everything to survive. I also started with a walker, a stick and the simple P.T. exercises that I did in school because I could not stand on my own. Constantly repeated painful exercises made me walk again. It was awful in those days, but I knew if I had to walk again, this was the only way.

This virtue of perseverance is the hallmark of all great achievers on this planet. "If you wish success in life, make **perseverance** your bosom friend, **experience** your wise counsellor, **caution** your elder brother, and **hope** your guardian genius" – so said, Joseph Addison. The biggest prison is made within our minds by our own regressive attitudes. We give up easily and begin comparing ourselves with others. Instead, we should surround ourselves with people who are inspired by life. They do more than the ordinary and are in a constant state of hunger to learn more and more. Be different, do different, and then you shall be at the top of the world. It does not matter if we don't make it all the time – actually, if we pursue various activities, the impact of the failure is less. Besides, we did what we did then with what we knew about how to do it. Now that we know better, we can do better. Life comes with its inevitable trials and tribulations - do we always want a straight jacket life? To live only for results would be to sentence oneself to confinement of the mind, while the wide-open oceans of learning, experience and endeavour remained unexplored. My only sure reward is in my actions and not from them.

So what is persistence?

A quote by Calvin Coolidge aptly sums up the quality of persistence:

"Nothing in the world can take the place of Persistence. Talent will not; nothing is more common than unsuccessful men with talent. Genius will not; unrewarded genius is almost a proverb. Education will not; the world is full of educated derelicts. Persistence and determination alone are omnipotent. The slogan 'Press On' has solved and always will solve the problems of the human race."

The definition of persistence is: "Refusing to give up or let go"; the word is derived from the word "persist", which means to endure: to remain: to continue: to last:

Persistence is "consistency, steadiness and tenacity".

Persistence is continuing even in adverse circumstances, failing, learning and doing it again until one succeeds in the endeavour.

Whenever you think of giving up, remember how children learn to walk by falling, getting up, falling, getting up until finally step by step, they learn to walk on their own Persistence.

Understand Persistence.

Most people are persistent in certain areas of their personality which is fun to do and which they like to do repeatedly, but persistence is not about what we like to do – it is about accomplishment or goal achievement.

I like to sing - persist.

I hate to get up early for a morning walk - persist.

Persistence is a thought pattern that transforms into a habit. Persistence can help us to achieve success, and we may even start to like our dislikes.

So let us start now.

Becoming Persistent

- **Become constant or be consistent** with exercising the discipline of consistency. Start your day with 'things to do' and do them and start increasing the degree of difficulty. Your own discipline will give you more self-esteem and win over the respect of others.

- **Use Tenacity.** Even in constant failure doing it again and again ultimately results in success.

- **Endurance**: Failures are lessons towards victory. Endurance is strength, tolerance and patience - so endure, persist and win.

Persistence will help in positive conditioning for achieving goals and finally living a successful life.

Are you not getting an opportunity?

Failed many times?

Afraid to do it again?

Persist!

- **Decide what you want to accomplish and set goals**. We all know how important it is to set goals for achieving success in any endeavour, so take some time to figure out what it is you want to achieve. Years ago, researchers surprisingly found that people who set clear, concise goals succeeded in achieving 95% of the time! Interestingly, it also emerged that they only achieved their goals if they refused to quit and continued to bounce back from difficulties along the way.

- **Prepare for Obstacles and Setbacks**. Know and accept that there will be obstacles and setbacks; then prepare for them. Nothing important was ever accomplished without adversity, setbacks and difficulties to contend with along the way. Henry Ford went bankrupt three times before he managed to design his first automobile. As we all know and are grateful for, he subsequently succeeded in becoming one of the richest men in the world. He said: "Failure is merely an opportunity to begin again more intelligently." Thomas Edison is said to have tried 10,000 times to create the light bulb before he succeeded.

People who have persisted in spite of Disabilities and Obstacles:

- Ludwig van Beethoven (composer, pianist) became deaf at the age of 30 and composed most of his famous works after he lost his hearing.

- Helen Keller (author) was deaf and blind from the age of 19 months. She wrote 12 books, various articles and was the first blind person to receive a Bachelor of Arts degree.

- John Milton, the famous poet, was blind when he wrote Paradise Lost.

- James Earl Jones (actor), known for his booming, resonant voice, was once a stutterer.

- Terry Fox (runner) was an amputee from cancer.

One of the ways you can prepare for setbacks and obstacles is to anticipate potential problems and have a contingency plan.

Also keep in mind that when we are overwhelmed with a problem or difficulty, we don't have time to develop the persistence necessary to deal with the particular obstacle or set back. However, if we plan in advance for life's inevitable ups and downs, we will be psychologically ready when they come upon us.

- **Take the first step**. You cannot persevere - much less succeed - if you never try to accomplish something. So many of us procrastinate due to fear of failure or are too frozen in our tracks to take the first step towards achievement. You will not fail if you don't try something; however, you will never succeed either. As the popular saying goes, "The only real failure in life is the failure to try."

- **Review, re-evaluate and revise**. If things do not work out the way, you hoped then review the steps you took and the process you followed. Re-evaluate by examining what went wrong and where. What didn't it work? What could you have done better? Did you have all the necessary skills and tools? Your findings will be most illuminating, and in turn, allow you to set up a better, more comprehensive approach for the next attempt. You will revise and improve the current strategy.

- **Garner support and encouragement**. Stay away from people who do not encourage; instead, seek advice from those experienced in your field of endeavour and those who want you to succeed. They can assist you by making suggestions and recommendations based on their experience and expertise. You will still have to do the hard work, but there is nothing more encouraging than having positive inputs.

- **Maintain focus.** One of the obstacles to attaining success is losing motivation and focus. A good way to maintain focus is to visualize yourself accomplishing your goal no matter what it takes. Vividly see yourself accomplishing your goal – keep your eye on the prize. Likewise, avoid getting caught up in negative or unproductive thinking such as, "This will never work." "I can't do this." Instead, keep inspiring slogans handy, pictures of those who have persevered in life, and whatever else will motivate and boost your drive.

In personality development, persistence is used to develop all our physical and psychological needs. It helps in positive conditioning in achieving goals and having a successful life. We need to reinforce the belief that Till I SUCCEED, I WILL PERSIST.

- **Enjoy!** The greatest feelings of accomplishment derive from knowing you've done it!

And now, a penny for your thoughts!

1. How can you become persistent? --------------

----

2. What is the role of persistence in personality development?-------------------------------

3. List any four areas where you would like to be more persistent --------------------------

   How will you do it? -----------------------------

   ----

4. How would being persistence benefit me? --

   ----

5. What are satisfying answers to life's persistent questions? -----------------------------------

6. Is persistence relevant for you? This depends on your age and requirement so Why is a big question you need to find out.

7. How long will it take to chalk out your path toward being resolute?

8. If you fail intermittently then would you give up your resilience?

9. Do you possess enough mental strength to continue?

10. How will perseverance prepare you for the future? Also, how would you define resilience?

CHAPTER FOUR

EMBARKING ON A MEANINGFUL JOURNEY

No matter what I do, I have one central question that drives my work. How can we live a useful life that matters? I believe that a productive life equals happy and fulfilling life. Life is beautiful but not always easy, and the challenge lies in facing them with courage, letting the beauty of life act as a balm. Difficulties test courage, patience, perseverance and the true character of a human being. It is only when one toils and sweats it out that success is nourished and sustained. Everyone takes each step in a very unique way; similarly, at each moment in the journey of life, you are presented with an opportunity to react differently. It is better to be a lion for a day than a sheep all your life. You may even make the same choices over and over again because you do not know how to choose otherwise. I am always doing things I can't do - for me, it is a series of baby steps. Nobody grew up with constant emotions - life is a game, and there are no mistakes but only lessons to learn. I strongly believe that our lives begin to end the day we become silent about the things that matter.

A small encounter with the extraordinary comes to my mind, when I met 96-year-old

Dr Niren Chakraborty, an MBBS Graduate of Calcutta Medical College during the 2019 Durga Puja Celebrations in Kolkata. I was amazed to see him beat all others in a conch-blowing competition in the open category consisting of competitors up to one-fourth his age! I further found that he had been winning this competition for the last five years. He, in fact, broke his own record that year with an astounding timing of 40 seconds!

Life is a lifetime challenge - you are successful if you feel the contentment and you know it in your heart that you made it in a good way. Sometimes the opportunities are really not meant for you, so strive to recognize the correct path. Too much love and hatred creates an imbalance, so never give up on what you believe in. Life is not always fair - just like the caterpillar does all the work, but the butterfly gets all the publicity. Do not be afraid of change by letting go - it is not a negative thing; it is creating a new life.

My journey as a coach has so many options. I may have come on a different ship, but we are in the same boat now, with goals to reach, people to meet. There will be times where you may not know what you want, who you want, or where you want to go. In these moments we must always remember, the best choice is standing still. You can't go back and change the beginning but can start where you are and change the ending. Actually, I read a quote which, in essence, said, *"To succeed in life you need three things – a wishbone, a backbone, and a funny bone"*. The Good, the Bad and the Ugly that I have left in the past remains in the past - I have no regrets about that. I am ready to embrace the brand new beginning of my life as a coach to transform life for as many as I can.

Why we should have a meaningful life is because our energy when invested in fruitful and constructive actions gives us so much joy and fulfilment that we become powerful within because we look outward to create and develop. If you take human life on a scale of hundred, the first 20 years we are discovering ourselves, the last 20 years are unknown - it is the time in between that matters.

What are we doing about it? Are we letting it pass by or living it?

To have a meaningful life:

1. How do you manage emotions ----------

2. Are you self-motivated--------

3. Do you make up with people who annoy you ------

4. Do you challenge yourself -----

5. Do you encounter obstacles daily---- keep a record.

6. How would you describe yourself ------

7. What holds you back-----

8. Do you like who you are------

9. What would you like people to say about you if they were asked in a gathering -----

10. What would you regret in life--------

CHAPTER FIVE

LIVING BEYOND THE ORDINARY

Do you usually acknowledge the beauty in everyday moments? Are you in sync with an awakened sense of all your senses – seeing, hearing, smelling, touching, tasting as much of the world as you can and appreciating all you discover? If so, you're someone living with what philosopher Bertrand Russell calls 'zest'.

> *"Without zest, what is life?*
> *Just waiting for death?"*
>
> **—Rajneesh**

Life could never be complacence to a person who has inculcated the habit of zest – in other words, for someone who lives with attentive curiosity to the details of life. A common factor among all happy people is "living with zest".

You know you are living with zest if you purposefully notice the details of the route to wherever you are going, or you choose some items because you love their texture and their feel, or you pick a soap or a product because you love its fragrance - smell being as important to you as the item. Do you ever notice the fairy lights that make different patterns; are you likely to notice the interesting shadow you create while walking –

sometimes long and sometimes short or even fat and obese, or a beautiful pattern created on the table cloth by a lamp; or how the stars are shaped like a bear or search for the Orion in the sky on a starry night? Do you hear the music in public places and start humming the tune - sometimes recommending it to people; or notice the way people speak - whether they have friendly voices or interesting tones and accents - which then makes you inquisitive about them? Are you the kind of person who can recognize some faces whom you do not know - recognize them as you see them around on a daily basis - like the people waiting in the bus queue everyday or also the people whom you see in the office canteen.

It is said that we all experience about 20,000 individual 'moments' in a day. If you are able to admire more of these moments in time instead of letting them go by without capturing them in the panorama of your memory, you are optimizing your joy in the present, just like the butterfly which counts the moments and not the years. People who have a lot of fond memories and precious moments stored in their minds are people living with zest. The less the number of memories you have in life, the more you are whizzing past your life. The beautiful poem by the Welsh poet WH Davies aptly expresses it in the poem called 'Leisure'. The poem was published in the year 1916 when the poet predicted in his thoughts the predicament of modern life as we see it today. The message is that our busy lives have made us insensitive towards beautiful nature that surrounds us as we speed by our lives and never ponder to soak in our surroundings which can give us so much joy and satisfaction to live life to its fullest. The poem goes thus:

"What is a life full of care,
We have no time to stand and stare.
No time to stand beneath the boughs
And stare as long as the cows.
No time to see, in broad daylight,
Streams full of stars, like the skies at night.
No time to turn at the Beauty's glance,
And watch her feet, how they can dance.
No time to wait till her mouth can
Enrich that smile her eyes began.
A poor life this is if, full of care,
We have no time to stand and stare."

—**William Henry Davies**

If you want to enjoy your life more, you can begin by living and loving more of it by zestfully with every little gorgeously detailed moment in life.

Inculcate the habit of zest purposefully; seek out beauty in all seemingly trivial moments of existence; the texture, taste and aroma of the food you eat and the interesting faces of the people travelling on the bus with you. You will not only experience more happiness on a daily basis but also cherish more happy memories when you look back on your life. So -

"Let us be up and doing

Life is not an empty dream

Act, act in the living present!

For, life is real! Life is earnest!"

Sit back and reflect a moment:

What are your small moments of joy?

Why is a zest for life so important for life?

What are you passionate about?

Write down five people whom you admire and why?

If you were to draw a picture depicting your life, what would you draw?

CHAPTER SIX
SUCCESS BUILD-UP

> *"In life, lots of people know what to do,*
> *but few people actually do what they know.*
> *Knowing is not enough! You must take action!"*

— **Tony Robbins**

Be what you are and know what you really want. You have to know your own strengths and weaknesses and try to enhance what you are good at and concentrate on the minuses to improve along with what you are good at. This introspection will give a clear picture of your way to success.

Do the things you do the best to start with.

Have a life oriented around what is important to you; spend time with your family and friends.

Lead a life with financial gains which will help you in doing what you love to do most.

So first to Be and then Do; rewards will automatically follow. When we start looking outward, things start moving.

We need to do away with things that drain us; we tolerate so many things at a time, and that drains our energy; start feeling light. The physical, mental, and emotional clutter holds us back and is a huge drain in energies needed for our drive to success. When we are light and clutter-free, we can create space for thinking and creativity.

Next, we should focus on our energy - what kinds of signals we are sending, are they positive or negative?

Surround yourself with people who give positive vibes and make yourself so vibrant that people get attracted to you. Always spread positive energy to get what you want. Always ask what you can do differently - keep reinventing yourself all the time.

For just five minutes a day, listen to your inner self and understand what signals it is giving you. Most successful people will tell you that they have a 'me' time for themselves every day.

Your body also gives you signals - it gives messages and clues all the time about what is going on with you. One easy way to know is how you are breathing - is it shallow or is it full. If it is shallow, then you are in stress.

It is very important to have a fun time with like-minded people - a lot of creative ideas start flowing in such gatherings. Also if you have some hobbies like reading or writing which you may have given up, restart to enjoy doing what you love doing again.

When you decide to create time by managing time, you will realize how much time you have to do things without having to rush through. Enable yourself to be at least ten to fifteen minutes early than even a minute late. If you can achieve this, you will see that you also have time to relax apart from having catered for unforeseen delays.

During our Air Force days whenever we had to go to official parties my husband and I would always be waiting at the car park a few minutes before so that we could enter the hall at the exact time.

It is vital to postpone activities which can wait; delegate or simply to let go when creating time for yourself.

Communicate successfully – how many times have we all felt that if we had used better words or tone or waited for that opportune moment, results of the interaction gone by could have been so much more fruitful. I have faced all these situations with family members as well as at work. Mastering communication is a process which takes a lot of practice.

In a situation while talking if there are two sides you, you have to own the perspective you believe in - you need not always say what other person wants to hear. However, at the same time, you must be able to sense how far you can go, and not go beyond that limit. In case you are angry, do not react instantly or emotionally, but rather allow yourself to cool down to a neutral state of mind and then get back to the conversation. It is always better to have two-way communication than one of the parties not participating at all. Too much of probing can put off a communication.

One has to be methodical and analytic in one's quest for success. One of the methods you can adopt is to draw a circle of life as it is at present, where you can put down which areas of your life need more attention, viz. finance, relationship, health, alone time, leisure, hobby, personal growth and assign values to them on a scale of 0 to 10. See how you fare. It is most likely that you will be able to define and identify the areas that need enhancement. Create such a mind map of the area in your life. Make a goal list of what you want to tackle first. Write down something that you want and then visualize methods which could be adopted to attain it, and then take resolute action.

Everyone needs people around to support and motivate us to create a circle of influence so that while we progress, towards our goal, they are there to support, motivate and validate us.

Create a vision board with five a year goal and write down date wise what you will achieve in the first year and break it up into quarters so that even if they overlap you can still complete them within that year. Regularly check your progress - a daily 'things to do' will help accomplish the task faster. Write down a happy note to yourself or share it with the circle of influence and family - they would always be supportive about your goal.

A small exercise of recalling your feats and achievements from your childhood till date and ticking and matching the goals achieved from the vision board will keep you motivated.

It is good for the growth of civilization that human beings constantly strive to gain greater and greater rewards, for it is this urge, this ambition, this aspiration that moves men and women to bestir themselves to greater levels of achievement.

"Individual success is to be won in most instances by studying and diagnosing the kind of rewards human hearts seek today and are likely to seek tomorrow."

—**B.C. Forbes**

Procrastination as a form of behaviour generally occurs when we are not excited about the work, or the work is unmanageable or if one is not capable. You often do not realize that you are delaying decisions, and this is because we often do not listen to warnings of our inner self when it reminds us repeatedly that time is ticking by. We choose to procrastinate, and suddenly we get overwhelmed when we realize that time has run out and scramble at the last minute to finish what we had set out to do. We need to identify and ensure reaching milestones in time in our journey to success. Sometimes we need help to complete our task - do seek help from others who know better than you -there is no shame in seeking help.

Trust yourself and take calculated risks - success often has more to do with courage than anything else - moving out of your comfort zone and stepping into the unknown. You may suddenly discover that you are enjoying it and your hidden talents come out. Living your own success is what you should be looking for, not someone else's success even if you are taking someone's help for a while to launch yourself. But ultimately, you have to break free to create your own identity.

Your dream should inspire you to stop only when you have achieved it - so go on till you find fulfilment and joy and start living your dream.

Thank God for His blessings and whatever you have got in life, because many others may not have what you have. Even if others seem to have more than you, you do not know their actual story. Some of the blessings can be as simple as good health, having good friends and family.

What is your relationship with money? Money is not intrinsically bad as it gives security, spending power to pursue want you to want to do and also to support many organizations who are working for the benefit of mankind. You can be a contributor to these causes, and for that, you need to have prosperity, consciousness and enjoy your philanthropic activities.

When you acknowledge others who have helped you grow, it makes them grow too. As I had said earlier, when your work is aligned with your values and talents, it becomes meaningful, and you start loving what you are doing.

You need to go on holidays to rejuvenate and de-clutter your mind and body, where you can relax and enjoy bringing out the child within you.

We need to think about ourselves first instead of pleasing others - learn to please yourself first. We need to understand our emotions and monitor our thoughts and be open to possibilities.

Finances play a great role in our lives - it is always advisable to learn to manage it well.

Resources need to be fully utilized if up-gradation of technology is required to ease your work - it is worth investing in it.

Success build-up is possible when you have a burning desire, and you are self-motivated with a strong intention, commitment, support of influence around you, action steps in place, ready to reinvent, rediscover and ready to fine-tune your actions as required. Recognize success and learn from what did not work.

Never ever be scared of competition and comparison - consider yourself unique in your own way.

Be bold – do not allow others to pull you down; stretch yourself as much as you can; start practising every day little by little. Work towards excellence and do not bother too much to be a perfectionist. Wear a smile from your heart and work towards your success because your body language and posture will generate positive thinking.

"Where body language conflicts with words that are being said, the body language will usually be the more 'truthful' in the sense of revealing true feelings."

—Glen Wilson

The main thing above everything is what is it that you really want out of life? Put yourself in a state that you are always achieving success and fulfilment and reflect after a period of time, all that you have achieved and trim the loose end and rejoice.

To end, I would like to say that maintaining a positive out outlook is to appreciate and feel thankful for all the good things in your life. So go ahead and start writing down your gratitude and appreciation for things and people in your life and surroundings.

When I visited Pondicherry, I had picked up a book from the Sri Aurobindo Ashram - Stories Told by the Mother. One of the stories called 'Virtues' is so profound that I would like you all to read it. I have therefore reproduced it below.

The Virtues

A Tale for Young and Old

Once upon a time, there was a splendid palace, in the heart of which lay a secret sanctuary, whose threshold no being had ever crossed. Furthermore, even its outermost galleries were almost inaccessible to mortals, for the palace stood on a very high cloud, and very few, in any age, could find the way to it.

It was the palace of Truth.

One day a festival was held there, not for men but for very different beings, gods and goddesses great and small, who on earth are honoured by the name of Virtues.

The vestibule of the palace was a great hall, where the walls, the floor, the ceiling, luminous in themselves, were resplendent with myriad glittering fires. It was the Hall of Intelligence. Near to the ground, the light was very soft and a beautiful deep sapphire hue, but it became gradually clearer towards the ceiling, from which inverted buttercups of diamonds hung like chandeliers, their myriad facets shooting dazzling rays.

The virtues came separately but soon formed congenial groups, full of joy to find themselves for once at least together, for they are usually so widely scattered throughout the world and the worlds, so isolated among so many alien beings.

Sincerity reigned over the festival. She was dressed in a transparent robe, lie clear water, and held in her hand a cube of purest crystal, through which things can be seen as they really are, far different from what they seem, for there, their image is reflected without distortion.

Near to her, like faithful guardians, stood Humility, respectful and proud, and courage, lofty-browed, clear-eyed, his lips firm and smiling, with calm and resolute air.

Close beside Courage, her hand in his stood a woman, completely veiled, of whom nothing could be seen but her searching eyes, shining through her veil. It was Prudence.

Among them were Charity, at once calm and vigilant, active yet discrete as she passed through the groups a soft light spread through her inseparable companion, her twin sister Justice. Around Charity thronged many shining escorts, Kindness, Patience, Gentleness and many others.

But then suddenly, at the golden threshold, a newcomer appears. With great reluctance, the guards have agreed to admit her. Never before they have seen her and there was nothing in her appearance to impress them. She was very young and slight, and the white dress she wore was very simple, almost poor.

She takes a few steps forward with a shy, embarrassed air apparently ill at ease to find herself in such a large and brilliant company. She pauses, not knowing towards whom she should go. After a brief exchange with her companions, Prudence goes towards the stranger. Then clearing her throat, as people do when they are embarrassed, she turned to her and said, "We who are gathered here and know each other by our names and our merits, are surprised at your coming, for you appear to be a stranger to us. We do not seem to have ever seen you before. Would you be so kind as to tell us who you are?" Then the newcomer replied with a sigh, "Alas! I am not surprised that I appear to be a stranger in this palace, for I am rarely invited anywhere. My name is Gratitude."

"Feeling gratitude and

Not expressing it is like

Wrapping a present and

Not giving it."

—**William Arthur Ward**

Why is practising gratitude and appreciation so important in life?

You will know if you start writing out the situations and events that made a difference in your life.

1. What made you laugh today?

2. What did you witness recently, that reminded you that people are good?

3. Was today better than yesterday?

4. What did I learn today?

5. What was the one small victory we had today?

6. What is the difference between gratitude and appreciation?

7. What simple pleasure you can enjoy today?

8. How do your friends show that they care about you?

9. Has someone helped you recently?

10. Do you thank people on a daily basis like the auto driver, etc.?

CHAPTER SEVEN

SPINNING IN SUCCESS

*"Some are born great; some achieve greatness,
And some have greatness thrust upon them."*

—*Twelfth Night* (William Shakespeare)

In life, many a time we tend to take the easier route to success even though we know that something is not correct, but we never voice our opinion out of an apprehension of antagonizing others. The world is changing all around us with modern technology. Each era with a new beginning gives us the opportunity to acknowledge success and take up challenges.

People become great when they live and die for some cause which is greater than their own aspirations. Even if one cannot do much for the cause, the very nature of a just cause discourages apathy and draws people to it. We need to ask ourselves, are we a uniting factor for causes or a dividing one. Can we say that we play a positive role, that our attitudes are positive and have a sense of self-satisfaction and self-esteem?

Does your happiness depend on your choice only, because you want to be a part of the issue, or is it because you just want to "follow the crowd", so to say? This is important in the human context because unlike other creations, we have the intellect and freedom of choice. We may not be able to choose our circumstances in life but can make our own decisions based on our own sense of right or wrong.

Every person has hidden possibilities which are often undiscovered. When we overcome the weakness of failure and realize that life as a whole is very valuable and that if one part fails it does not mean that the whole is a failure, we could say that we have attained some form of enlightenment. We need to block ourselves against an overbearing negative attitude.

A person can re-invent and make life fruitful; possibilities can be turned into success and problems into a stepping stone. Character and attitudes can thus be re-defined as a positive step towards success, and with success, life can go beyond death. You can become a new you and dreams can be achieved. A person's value system needs to be strong and can be weaved into faith to enhance the possibility of success.

Striving for success can be a result of inner growth. There is no need to push and shove to reach the pinnacle. We do not work to finish the task but to do it well and to enjoy every step in its progress. Each person is unique, and it is imperative to develop that as an individual if you are a worthwhile person, a capable person and a good human being. When you achieve success material gain follows automatically - it becomes the by-product. Perseverance is the key to success - the person who wins is the same one who never gives up. You have to be smart and intelligent to seize the opportunity to achieve success. Being born rich is not necessary to achieve success. There are people with disabilities like Helen Keller or people who rose from abject poverty like Henry Ford and Abraham Lincoln. They all had to fight against odds and make a success of their lives.

You can become a success in more than one field by your inner traits and attributes. A splendid example is that of Leonardo da Vinci – painter, sculptor, engineer, mathematician and philosopher. You can change your path if the one you are following at the moment is not working - you could channelize your efforts to do something different.

'You need to love yourself' may sound selfish, but then who will love you if you do not love yourself. You have to look after and train our mind, body, soul, emotions and have to take charge of your life so that you do not feel ignored or embarrassed any more. Spend time with people who have achieved this stage. Reconfirm that you are neither better nor worse than any other in the world and have equal priority to the divine right to live a life of dignity and worth in this world. We cannot live up to someone else's expectations or vision from the time we are born. We have always been taught to live our lives by the way the world tells who we should be, what our life should be. But in truth the fact is that we are what we are with our inherent individuality and we should have our own style and approach for life and living - no one else can be who you are.

Share your life and success with others – with that you would enrich your own lives and that of others. Caring and sharing give great satisfaction. When we go beyond our physical capacity and live for something better and bigger, then and then only, you become highest you.

To spin in success, we need to develop our attitude towards self-evaluation and motivate ourselves towards doing something meaningful. Soon after a child is born, he/she starts to learn the approved patterns of behaviour of the society into which the child is born and brought up, and likewise, one person learns from the other. Attitudes are learned through life experience, and thus the behaviour pattern of the individual is formed and creates a value system and beliefs of the person and makes him act in a particular way. The person is, so to say, 'prototyped'. This status can hardly power excellence or brilliance or 'super-success'. To achieve such heights, there must be a trace of the maverick in you - a certain extra-ordinary deviation from the ordinary. This requires extra effort along with proper intervention, guidance and determination. Before you think of becoming great, you have to think yourself as an entity apart from the ordinary, ensconced on the loftiest crest, impeccable - in other words, seeing yourself with new eyes, growing to the highest level, without having to prove anything to anybody, self-actualized, exhibiting steadfastness of purpose, confidence and a sense of inner pride. You will gain mastery in anything which you want to do if you advance confidently in the direction of your own dreams and endeavour to lead the life you have always wanted to. A confident person masters art of being at the level of his or her perceived life and destiny and the attainment of lifelong dreams.

Success is also a direct consequence of the value that you give to your time and how fruitfully you spend it. The present is the only time you will ever have - if you use up the present in mere planning, calculating, wishing and dreaming of a golden future, the future can never come up to your expectations. If you always live in dreams of the future, it becomes the only purpose of life. Thinking about the future and planning is necessary, but for that, the action has to start now, logically and realistically. Who wants to live in absentia? You have to stop idealizing the future and take action now to be able to achieve it, no matter at what age or in which stage you are. The trap of future needs to broken by beginning to live fully today - it is a skill which we have to develop by cherishing the past fondly and learning lessons from past mistakes so as not to repeat them, but then you also need to say goodbye to the past and live in the present, working towards the goals of the future - it is an attitude that one has to inculcate.

Thinking is considered as what makes us human, and ability makes us elevate ourselves beyond being ordinary. Some feel trapped and cannot control their situation because they are unable to make correct choices, resulting in self-defeating thoughts emerging from their own minds which choke their effort to break free. As your thoughts are your own creation, do not fear them but rather accept, understand and use the genesis of their birth for course corrections and greater impetus in your efforts for self-actualization. Once the understanding is clear that emotions and thoughts are linked to the perception of your level of success or failure, you will be able to understand them better be ready to have that attitude to tackle with success all circumstances or hurdles that you may have to face in the future.

Identifying instincts and intuitions also contributes to success. Our ability to know ourselves comes from learning how to consult our inner ability then developing the confidence of relying on it completely. If we feel that external rewards are controlling us and our efforts and clashing with internal signals, then we must know that we allowed it to happen.

Keep a few things in mind:

We need to create our own identity.

The need for self-respect and respecting others is fundamental to every human being.

Human beings do not function well without a sense of belonging.

Being loved and needed is also a primary requirement of a person.

The need to feel productive and useful is very crucial.

You must relax and have Buzz moments with your friends and family or even by yourself.

There is no need for conformity all the time.

You must pay heed to your own sense of Justice.

Make a special effort to find the truth in any matter.

There is a need to seek out information for decision-making.

We need to cultivate a sense of purpose and meaning in life - without it, we would feel empty and unfulfilled. There is no need to impress anyone else - the more you are yourself, the more likely you will feel purposeful and significant in your life. Do not settle for less than you might become. If you know yourself and you are conscious of your core beliefs, and they are in line with your purpose, effort and drive, you are a winner because it is a reality and a condition which gives you the attitude and ability to think of yourself as a winner. Be confident that you can achieve great success by relying on yourself. This state energizes your subconscious mind, which accepts that picture and propels your conscious mind to make it come true. Have the confidence to believe that nothing can get you down permanently and that even if you face a temporary setback, you will bounce back again and again.

It is said that we continue doing many things until we find that which gives us joy and happiness and a sense of fulfilment. We do this often in spite of apparently having everything - we go on seeking such moments interminably because inside us the soul needs to be eternally satisfied and once it is happy we look for another source of fulfilment. We need to step up our inner power which can do incredible things which sometimes people call miracles. Never think down, but always look up as the Almighty moulds life exactly as deservedly it should be. Rekindle the positives and life-sustaining enthusiasm always, and never indulge in gloomy thoughts. One has to try a lot, spend a lot of effort before we can deserve to achieve success.

In difficult situations, if everything fails, you still have You left. Believe that there is an answer to every problem, and there is a solution. There is no need to force an answer; keep your mind relaxed - tension blocks off the logical thought process. Solutions will come. Think and analyze the situation - solutions will come to you clearly. We often let our emotions cloud our judgment. When you encounter problems become logically analytic. Do not start with a presumption of who is wrong but try to analyze what is wrong and where you are at this moment. Do listen to your inner signals - assess the thoughts and receive the invaluable divine guidance of your inner self. Visualize success and achievements because creative spiritual thinking has an amazing power to give you the right answers.

Take the advice of your coach and mentor, but take life and problems in your own hands. Great energy exists in the human mind, and with its potential, an average individual is capable of much greater achievements than he can realize. Develop a strong mental shield to ward off negative feelings, for "tough times never last, but tough people do". Believe in God and in yourself. Never react emotionally - use logic and the intuition of your inner self to react and pro-act. Trials and tribulations are there to test our mettle. Always believe that you can take it, you can make it, and you will find out that you definitely can. If you can think about failures, then you can certainly think about success for your own benefit. You must always think that you can.

Some tips towards success build-up:

Build up calmness of mind by thinking calm thoughts and talking calm words.

Build up a source of constant energy.

Build up emotional stability.

Build up a belief that the best is yet to happen.

When you are clear in your mind what you want to achieve in life and devote yourself wholeheartedly to it, then only the best can happen.

Positivity of attitude teaches us not to reject an idea or a possibility outright.

Detach from things and people that enslave you and limit your freedom.

We do things better when we put our heart into it - we need to trust our gut feeling.

Watch the words that we use.

Dream big dreams.

Work big - there are no hard and fast rules to success - only hard work.

Eliminate excuses.

Let go of a day - even if you have made blunders just let go because tomorrow is a new day.

Know your inner self - success has come even to people with certain kinds of limitations.

Take stock of your life and play well - plenty of opportunities are waiting for you to make use of them.

In the end, I quote Rumi, the famous Persian Sufi Mystic:

"Mature Yourself.
No mirror ever became iron again.
No bread ever became wheat.
No ripened grape ever became sour fruit.
Mature yourself and be secure from a change
for the worse. Become light."

—Rumi

In other words, LIVE BEYOND THE ORDINARY!

To spin in success

1. How would you treat others normally?

2. How can you change yourself to be the person you want to be?

3. Name some positive attitudes you will cultivate in your life?

4. Name some positive affirmations you will use in your everyday life?

5. What kind of visualization will you consciously give the mind every day?

6. Do I control my thoughts in regards to my life?

7. Do I have unrealistic expectation from life?

8. Can I cultivate peace of mind whenever I feel annoyed?

9. How do I spend my Buzz moments?

10. Do I rigidly stick to my views, or am I tolerant of other people's views and opinions that are different from mine?

CHAPTER EIGHT

FITNESS OF MIND AND BODY

"The human body is the best picture of the human soul."

—Tony Robbins

There are many definitions of happiness and pleasure - happiness we get from what we have done, whereas pleasure is felt in the act that we do. The mind can be rejuvenated with the kind of deeds we do if we interact with people positively. We live in the world with ourselves, but when we dive deep into the inner world, we discover our thoughts, feelings and actions which we need to exalt through meditation, yoga or in any pursuit of art painting, singing, playing games exercising any form of activity where we put our full concentration; where mind becomes one with the activity and the divine soul. When we do what we love and develop a cosmic consciousness and are aware of the thoughts, feelings and actions, our minds are elevated, and we realize a perennial flow of happiness.

Meditation and yoga is a process to forget one's self through techniques enabling an inward journey of the mind which has tremendous health and mental benefits, my favourite being laughter yoga. Can you laugh for no reason, actually you can, and that will make you feel much better. One should develop a sense of humour which is so uniquely human and appreciate the lighter side of life. It reduces stress and erases arrogance.

My fellow coach Kelsey de Waal from the Netherlands has shared with me few insights regarding meditation. She is an instructor and has this to say about rejuvenating your mind and body in regards to meditation.

Setting time for yourself in seclusion is mandatory to know what is going on in your body and mind. Meditation releases old pains which we are not aware of on a deep level. If the tension in mind is released, then the same happens for the body too. You become your own healer.

Meditation is the highest practice for self-development.

When you start your day by consciously focusing on yourself, your body and mind, you will be more conscious about what happens for the body too. You become your own healer.

Meditation is the highest practice for self-development.

When you start your day by consciously focusing on yourself, your body and mind, you will be more conscious about what happens around you and within you. You can feel, observe and let the feelings flow through you, instead of getting stuck or being controlled by your emotions and thoughts.

Meditation will not destroy thoughts or emotions. Nor, is it a very relaxed thing to do if you are a beginner. It requires consistent work. Relaxation is a byproduct. Thoughts will be there and emotions too. Your aim is to only increase the silent moments between the thoughts and feel your emotions fully. This results in better communication and expression towards others and yourself.

As a result, you get a 'clear' mind instead of an endless rattling mind. You will 'see' your thoughts and emotions and will be able to identify them as being helpful or harmful. In this way, you can consciously choose to 'listen' to what is happening within your mind. The more you practice that, the more your busy rattling mind becomes a great tool to work with.

However, a rattling mind, harmful thoughts or uncontrollable thoughts and emotions, can still be your 'experience' and also need to be embraced by you. Nothing is good or bad. The more you give your love or 'silent awareness' to everything that is within you, the more everything starts to settle down. Just watch. Be aware. Stay still as the deep ocean looking at her waves.

As your mind becomes clearer and you realize that awareness is all there is, you will become more productive and focused on the things you have to do. You also feel the emotions more clearly, and as a result, you can express yourself clearly about how you feel about a certain situation. You won't be occupied with unnecessary thoughts. Freedom from unnecessary thoughts will result in being more energetic throughout your day.

Your response towards external influences will not be a reflex or fear but a conscious act rooted in calmness and acceptance.

Ending the day with meditation clears your mind and gives room for new ideas to flow in like magic. You will wake up in the morning with new insights. These new ideas and deeper insights open up a gateway of possibilities. Meditation also gives you a tremendous amount of trust in the universe and a feeling of oneness. What are you willing to do to bring more consciousness into your life?

I meditate daily in the morning before breakfast and at night before sleep. Meditation is a ritual that you need to follow every single day.

There are many therapies to keep a person healthy and fit. Nature cure, a simple morning walk, cultivating good healthy habits, a good diet, all contribute towards healthy living, but above all, if you do what you love, like reading, writing, singing, dancing, travelling even meeting friends over a cup of coffee, can all boost up your quality of living. Just be happy - exercise, sleep, believe in lifelong learning. Physical and mental activity prolongs life. When we develop a passion to do something you do not need any talent - just be curious about things. Loving yourself and just being, you can go a long way.

Pujita Krishna, Founder and Artistic Director of Feet on Earth, Master's degree in Fine Arts and specializing in Dance from the University of California, and also an Indian Classical performer with expertise in Vilasini Natyam and Kuchipudi, has this to say -

Dance is a very visually appealing performing art, and Indian classical dance is all the more challenging because of its multi-faceted nature of encompassing all forms of arts within it- music, drama, literature and poetry. Furthermore, as an art form, it requires the practitioner to call upon every aspect of his/ her physical, emotional, intellectual and intuitive sensibilities to put together a package that captures the audience's hearts and minds.

There is much in dance that is challenging, at the same time gratifying. Learning a structured and formalised dance form requires tremendous discipline, both physical and mental. Unless you find yourself to pursue a certain regimen, you cannot improve upon your art and practice in the long term. Successful and renowned dancers both in the Indian and Western world of dance will vouch for that. This discipline and will power over a period of time engenders in the practitioner a certain mental, emotional and spiritual equilibrium. Studies have proven how dance prevents ageing and keeps the body and mind young. As a dancer who has studied various dance forms both Indian and global, I can say without the shadow of a doubt, that while dance is demanding, it is this very demanding nature of it that helps one find one's core.

I asked some of my friends what were the ways they tried to find relaxation other than the conventional ways - Sapna Agarwal, my fellow coach, wrote the following to me :

As I began writing my daily journal,

Laima came up to me, peeping into my dairy she inquisitively asked me,

Mama, you love writing the most?

Or do you love running more?

Or do you love deep breathing the most?

Her queries made me think,

Can I actually put a number or ranking on what I love the most?

I think I cannot.

As all these activities have a place and space in my life and none can replace the other in any way.

Laima left the room as her friend called her out for an evening doll play.

It sent an enquiry within me and I thought of penning down what it takes to lead a happy, fulfilling and enriching life for me.

Of course, we all have different avenues and areas and we explore and make them our source of ever lasting happiness.

One thing which is of utmost importance here is we can never derive or place our life's happiness on one object, person, hobby or passion.

What I feel is when all the areas of our lives come together into what we do at various levels make us happy and fulfilled.

Physical fitness / exercise (Running and strength work out) is one of them.

Humans were made to move, from our forefathers to the millennials now.

A lot has changed in how we deal with and see life but the elementary thing which can give you utmost joy and happiness is movement.

With the increase in our comfort levels and consumerism our need to move has reduced over time.

With this there is an ever increasing need to keep moving to maintain health and a basic standard of fitness.

Personally for me, I can never emphasize enough, running has been a great source of sustenance in the myriad hues of my life.

I feel I am a better human, mom, wife and daughter after I come back from a run.

The endorphin release is truly worth it.

But to each his own.

It can be Zumba for some, while others might find yoga and cycling to give them that nectar.

If I ask myself, is running that which sums up my source of joy alone?

Definitely not, I am a social being and love being with my friends and family.

The value of spending time on sweet nothings can never be enough - it is therapeutic to let your hair down when your friend circle makes you groove.

Similarly, with family around a sense of security and feeling of belonging keeps you warm and protected.

When you come back to your family after a hard day, it feels valuable.

At other times, when you enjoy or indulge in activities which make you forget the concept of time is very fundamental in bringing that rejuvenation back into your life .

Smelling lilies, sitting at the window side and enjoying a cup of hot coffee, reading the next best thriller, watching movies lying on the couch with a tub of popcorn, playing guitar or singing soulful melodies.

These are some of mine while others might have their own.

So often we get so caught up in the fast paced life that we forget to breathe.

We are always racing towards the next thing / project /meeting.

There is a never a dull or rather slow moment in our lives.

It is important to be fast but that we need to mindfully slow down too.

Slowing down doesn't mean we are losing it - it means we are sharpening our armoury for the task ahead of us - writing a daily journal, meditation, deep breathing, walk in the nature, just observing without thinking .

We are born multi-taskers without any iota of doubt but in performing our life's duties sometimes we end up becoming machines.

We are humans and we expect ourselves to not be one.

When we holistically look at quality of our lives, it shows us that being in the moment, living in the NOW is as much important as planning and building up your future.

I wake up early to gift myself the me time when I am my own company. When silence is peaceful as it allows me to set intentions for the day and reflect on my growth and experience my thoughts.

The hum drum of our daily life doesn't allow us to introspect .

It is important to invest in this time to bring organic growth in you as a human .

Meditation has helped me understand my true self as also allowed me to beat the stress which is a by-product of our competitive times.

Investment in learning a new hobby or simply taking up a course to upgrade your skills is also of paramount importance.

When we are open to learning, we grow.

Time is moving at lightning speed and with this there is ever increasing research, technology and invention.

It is only rightful to keep in tune with the time.

When we learn we can scale up our game and move forward.

I like learning new technology, reading new books, and at times taking up hobby courses.

What is therapy for someone might be irksome task for another.

It is individual choice and there can't be one formula that fits all.

Above everything that I have tried, the greatest and the most everlasting I have ever got is in expressing Gratitude.

Wherever I have been in my life, I have always felt grateful to God for getting me there.

There is a reason why we meet people, experience strange incidents or fall into traps.

We can't see explicitly what is the reason behind what happens.

I believe the higher self knows everything and it is always in our best interest.

Gratitude is a sure shot way to attract abundance in your life.

It is not in practicing Gratitude but in feeling it from the core of your being.

This difference is the game changer.

It brings me unfathomable joy.

I am thankful to Almighty and people around me for making me who I am today.

Life is not beautiful when you reach a destination but it's beauty is more often hidden in enjoying the process and in what the process makes you out to be .

Travel experience is also a therapy for the mind. I love to travel. After every trip, I come back totally rejuvenated in body and mind. On one such trip, I discovered a new me who could express myself in writing and read into peoples' minds and discover the way to rewire my mind.

"The world is a book and those who do not travel read only one page."

—Saint Augustine

My childhood was spent experiencing different smells of the soil of life due to the frequent transferable occupation of my parents. My childhood was spent experiencing different smells of the soil of life due to my father's transferable job – and just as the Earth moves around its own axis, I too joined in the spin, being married to a defence officer, and saw the sprawling deserts, roaring seas and the towering mountains all over India. Many lands with their distinct flavours thus shaped my formative years and early adulthood.

Travel became part and parcel of my life, and the thirst for travel became more and more pronounced as the years went by. Though I know that I cannot shrink the world, nor is it possible to visit all the places on this planet, a few items in a wish list always remained in my mind. Egypt was one such destination, but it always eluded me. After many years of planning and a strong desire to visit the land of the Pharaohs made me embark on the journey after meticulous planning, checking out many travel agents and advisers.

At last the day arrived when my husband and I boarded the Egyptian airlines, anxious in anticipation to see the land of my of dreams where I had fantasized that I was the pretty slave girl with raven hair giving water to the captive slaves who built those formidable pyramids - an overdose of historical and biblical cinemas that fanned my imagination.

We stepped out of the airport and were greeted by Iben, our guide, a Coptic Christian who would remain with us till the end of the cruise along the historical river Nile, and was already filling me up with stories of the early settlers and many historical facts in chronological order.

The days flew past in a panoramic whirl - it was a feast to the eyes and succour for the mind, while the vast expanse of the hot sun-kissed sands adorned by the majestic pyramids constructed with geometric precision, formed a tall backdrop beside the monolithic statues as the snub-nosed Sphinx stood sentinel over the city, looking down at us puny mortals. Flying along with the birds during the balloon ride we looked down at the valley of the kings and queens, trying to find the catacombs where lay the mighty pharaohs and their queens in eternal sleep - a land where death is evoked with reverence.

Every day the kaleidoscopic view of the land slowly unfolded its new mysteries which will be etched in my mind forever. The narrow alley-ways with their hookah bars, the salesmen are trying to entice the visitors with genuine and fake artefacts with equal gusto; the sparkling perfume jars of Abu Simbal, murals and frescos revelling the ancient history of Egypt, of their glorious victories and disastrous defeats. The sienna blue Mediterranean sea hugging the road where once the great Alexander rode his mighty horses, all came alive as if the history textbook came alive in front of my eyes. The serene Coptic churches, a treasure house of an ancient era, the ornate dome of the mosque were all a feast for the traveller's eyes. Ten days were not enough to capture the essence of the land.

The last evening of the journey drew near, sitting on the deck of the liner and seeing the mighty blue Nile dashing against the ship with an eternal lap, lap as if asserting its eternal presence and telling me so many tales of yore. I watched and wondered whether the fathomless Nile swelled up with tears of the slaves who toiled to build the wonders of the world - the majestic pyramids? Did the grand processions of the dead with their pomp and customary grandeur go to their final destination along this way? Maybe the queen of Egypt Cleopatra went for an evening sojourn in the Nile, and who did she accompany - the gallant warrior Mark Antony or the fearless conqueror Caesar? The oceanic river carried so many tales buried deep down; I wondered what sorrows or treasures it was hiding in its fathomless bosom?

As I heard the dinner gong I went down to the dining hall dressed in an Egyptian attire to attend the last supper for the guests - it was a grand local affair with a lavish spread of cuisines from different countries along with Egyptian drums and pipes playing for the graceful belly dancers doing the camel walk around the hall and dancing to their tune.

A sweet perfume of the lilies of the land and the aroma of the food with the din music and revelry gave a giddy feeling of excitement. My husband and I went to our table where our dining mates were waiting - a stocky American soldier with his Hellenistic looking Macedonian long-necked girlfriend. Every evening at dinner we would exchange our touring notes as they were with another travel agency. But this meeting was different as we bade farewell to familiar and to not so familiar faces, exchanged phone numbers and addresses knowing that we may never meet again.

We hurriedly packed our bags to board our flight back home - I felt as if we were the chosen few in Noah's arch and were going to our promised land.

When I settled down in New Delhi with my numerous bags full of souvenirs, gifts and a host of memories, I could not help comparing notes of two mighty civilizations so similar in many ways yet so unique in their own ways.

I lay back in a stupor, trying to sink in everything from the splendid journey. I could hear a far away repetitive tone of Miss George our teacher of history saying, "girls its Tu–tan–kamun and Nefreti and not Nefra-ti-ti" I could hear myself say aloud – "Miss, I just saw it all!" "Hey are you dreaming?", nudged my husband as I woke with a start and started rubbing my eyes – and would you believe what the first thing I saw was - a travel magazine and the same 'wanderlust' tempting me. How can I stay away from turning the pages of glossy pictures of unknown destinations? What will it be the mountains, desert or the sea the next time?

I know I have the travel bug. There are cures for many bugs that affect our health, but none for the travel bug and thank God for that.

As I was unpacking I knew I had a lot to do checking out travel agents, surfing the net, information from friends, scrounge and save, for I knew it would be the mountains next time.

After all, in the end, we only regret the chances we did not take.

CONQUERING WHISPERS IN THE HEAD

Whispers in the head are Intrusive thoughts that are unwanted and depressing in nature, inhibiting one's focus and application. They can be accompanied by distracting images, diverting people from their chosen path. You may be led to believe that you are lesser than you are, or your fortune does not favour you.

I often indulged in such thoughts due to instability that I experienced as a result of the transfers my husband faced during his active service in the Air Force. I had to pick up bits and pieces everywhere we went. To start and restart life over and over again often made me think that I had missed the bus, not knowing actually, this varied exposure was gradually filling up with experience, my previously inherent lack of exposure and knowledge.

Every time I would start to build my working life and bring it towards an upward swing, it would apparently collapse due to instability. I would get into depression, and unwanted thoughts would prevent me from achieving what I wanted out of life for myself. However, I gradually came to terms with myself and thought, "No, I have to do the best I can with whatever I have got", different opportunities started opening up. The acquired variety of experience and added qualifications picked up along the way fortified me to brace for the future.

One, therefore, has to understand the difference between the perceived situation and reality. We need to understand what are unwanted thoughts and that you, as a person, have not changed or become incapable. Those thoughts could be of fantasy, aggression or human relationships which may not always be supportive and often erode our self-confidence and belief in what the future could hold for us. Therefore,

- Learn to accept your thoughts
- Take the thoughts less personally
- Take the fear out of your thoughts, and
- Stop changing your appreciation of yourself and your destiny.

How to manage the whispers in your head?

Learning to accept one's thoughts is essential as otherwise, one would react emotionally and make oneself more unhappy and unable to cope with perceived disappointments adequately. We need to find ways of dealing with such thoughts by focusing on the constructive aspects of the situation so that the thoughts cannot disturb us. Constantly attention to negative perceptions only serves to strengthen them, often resulting in erosion of confidence and self-esteem, which could promote depression and a dangerous psychological situation. Acceptance helps to reduce the effects of those disturbing whispers in the head and change focus to more optimistic possibilities. With a positive mental outlook, negative thoughts cannot affect personalities or their future – they will come, and they will go – useless and unwanted as they are. If we keep those thoughts alive, we become fearful, uncertain and even over-react or react erroneously to situations. People's opinions become more important instead of your own confidence, resulting in a loss of self-esteem. This may make you start avoiding people and places that instigate your thought process and phenomena like anxiety and depression may take over your life. Conjured images of calamitous situations start controlling your response processes.

It is essential, therefore, to be able to deal summarily with negative thoughts and encourage strengthening of optimistic ones. We must listen to the little voice inside our head as our protector.

We are so caught up with the mundane affairs of life and living that we do not pay much attention to it, but the voice often does not go away. It can be a warning for us to take precautions in time - not to wait till some crisis occurs.

Therefore, we must train our own minds. Before we start our day, we must practice listening to our inner voice, reflect and meditate. We need to spend at least five minutes every day while breathing deep to listen to our voice and get a good start for the day. Our body also gives us messages and indications about what is going on with us - instead of ignoring it, we should pay heed to it.

I remember when I was doing sales and marketing for a timeshare company, I trained my mind to pick up correct signals with regard to sales while watching the body language of a person. Often my prediction came true when I listened to the voice inside my head. Your own body also often sends clues to make the right choice about what is going on in your life.

At the same time if the thoughts are cautioning and negative all the time, it can prevent you from functioning and taking the plunge to reach greater heights - it will lead you towards defeat. Anxiety due to unavoidable thinking can cause high blood pressure and nervousness and other such allied symptoms of mental stress. Unwanted thoughts must, therefore, be tackled carefully.

The best way to keep unwanted thoughts at bay is to practice breathing exercises.

Pray and dismiss worries by engaging in meaningful work to occupy the mind. Once in a while, it is good to write down your worries or tell your counselor, coach or a confidant about them so that your mind is relieved. Have a circle of good, caring people surround you most of the time.

It is very important to understand one's own thoughts. One has to make a conscious effort to control one's thoughts to convert them to positive whispers.

You need to find the answers to these questions yourself :

1. How can I manage whispers in our head?

2. Can I control my unwanted thoughts in a useful manner?

3. Can we manage emotions and keep ourselves motivated?

4. Where can we dump our negative thoughts and recognize the inner voice caution and control the one that pulls us back?

5. Can we learn to accept obstacles, doubts, mistakes?

I listened to my inner voice again and again, and it told me that I could not rebuild my future from the start, but I could certainly fight adversities and negative circumstances because life and success depend on the individual and not on the weighing scale of others. When your aspirations are realistic, and you are ready to work hard and change your thinking pattern, there is no looking back. Some time back, I had penned down a few lines when I used to be melancholy and how positive thinking changed my life:

There was life

Ennui crept over me insidiously,

That the moon was waning, my tea was cold.

A futile routine of home and work

Work and home;

That was life – glorious youth wasted in a meaningless drone

And a ceaseless hum

Of foolish joys and mundane sorrows.

I was a spider, weaving my web meticulously,

Not knowing why,

Never digressing;

The days lay like the blown flame of the forest blaze

With fire that was in them, now no more.

Ennui seeped through me –

A formless jigsaw of black and white.

But today the jigsaw fell into a pattern of a mosaic,

Every piece lay against each other.

The roadside Banyan had raised a shoot

And my heart had raised a song.

I have resurrected and as I looked around.

The bus conductor grinned and shouted

"Yelankha"!

A little girl smoothed her dress ;

A beggar stretched out his hands with a toothless grin ;

I smiled –

And there was life!

COMING ALIVE TO LIFE AND LIVING

Yes, that's me, 60 and counting; the beauty of the sunset of my life.

To the rest of the world, we are redundant -way past our shelf life - a little bit over the hill. I am talking about my impediments which you could relate to any of the barriers in your lives.

Young people forty and below live in their own island, with the rest shut off from them in an aged box. They often refer to us as seniors, not inability, but subtly reminding us of age, cutting you short while you are speaking as if you are from another galaxy. Young people make the world; they are the game-changers. Although perhaps I would not insist on competing with them, I certainly want my space and my moment in time. One of those moments came very recently, unpredictably, during the New Year party we were attending at the turn of the year, when the live band suddenly switched over from the monotonous rhythm of rock music to the ethereal strains of the Blue Danube and while we, the so-called Seniors, waltzed and twirled and swept across the dance floor, the younger generation was stumped. At the end of the number amidst thunderous applause, I could see the youngsters staring wide-eyed, and we just smiled and soaked it all in!!

When you grow up with full freedom, done it and seen it all from Jai Prakash Naryan to Modi - Jimmy Hendrix to Bon Jovi - Telegram to Face Time - remember that people born in the 50s and 60s are the flower children - Hippy cult, tattoo, grass and ecstasy. I thought life was a full cycle – then why should there be no space for seniors like us?

Time and tide wait for none - you have heard it a million times. How in a jiffy I changed from Didi to Auntyji - from salt and pepper hair to bifocals - the gradual physical transformation encompassed me while the heart and mind remained forever young. Inside I am petulant, capricious, demanding and why not? We suppress the urge to let go because of what people will say.

What should the so-called seniors do - curl up and await the sunset? This stereotype thinking needs to be broken by you all. 60 yrs and above need not spin endless tales to their grandchildren or laugh their lungs out at the corner of a park nor book a KRTC bus for the temple run for salvation.

When change is inevitable in life, you should embrace the jet setting, globe-trotting, club-hopping grand-parents. The grandchildren also have moved away from Grimm's Fairy Tales to the science fiction Harry Potter and to the stories of Geronimo, the analytical thinking mouse. No more do they indulge in playing Ludo but enjoy the thrills of the X Box.

Think about it - you all are going to be 3 to 4hrs older as you as you are reading my book. There is no escaping age, but one need not carry it like a shroud and lead a confined or isolated life. We all have lights within us, but we forget to switch them on. Everyone deserves a second chance - life need not be a big picture always, but it certainly can be a small framed picture too.

My take away at this age is how I deal with various emotions and the sense of self. Body and mind may not balance, but fantasy and dreams keep you going. Confidence and individuality give me the platform for diverse conversation; not being bored with something will always interest me in my ever-youthful mind. Have I lost something precious, or I am still searching for it or is it there for you to discover? Isn't life all about living? Can we not re-invent young and old? I prefer investing in fun time and talking freely and having people accepting me the way I am.

The chapters of life discover new passions as you go along the life-trek where someday somewhere you will find yourself, and that and only that can be the happiness or the bitterest hour of your life. Time is expensive - we have to put a value on it. It cannot always be 'play it safe'. As I look back, I have written my story, not saying good or bad but different.

I will never give in to old age until I become old. And I am not old yet. I read this beautiful quote which is so apt for me. People tend to make you feel that getting older is the worst thing that could happen, like a disease inflicting the world. This not true at all - there is no reason why, at an old age, you cannot be positive and live life to its fullest and have a grand time. This is the ideal time when with children having their own lives, the older generation is free to explore whatever they like and are not answerable to anybody and definitely not to peer pressure!

"My life, I realize suddenly, is July. Childhood is June, and old age is August, but here it is, July, and my life, this year, is July inside of July."

—Rick Bass

To sum up my journey of life, I am grateful to the Almighty for helping me achieve big and small victories in life which cannot be measured by others but means a lot to me. In the canvas of my life there may not be many masterstrokes, but plenty of long and short strokes which I have filled with colours, using brush, fingers, thumb and even the knife to scoop colours from the palate of life to sharpen the edges and leave deep impressions.

My canvas still has place left for adding some more. I often ponder whether I should use subdued hues to finish my paintings or should I splash vibrant colours of scarlet, red, midnight blue, golden yellow or royal violet? Is there any art critic reading my book? I wonder what you would have to say?

Happy Living!